PICKLEBALL

IS *Not* LIFE

PICKLEBALL IS GREAT.
GOD IS GREATER!

A 31-Day Bible Devotional that Includes Pickleball Tips & Strategies

Teresa Jungling

ISBN 979-8-218-26805-3
Copyright ©2023 PickleballMAX
P.O. Box 813
Mason, OH 45040

Dedication

This book is dedicated to all current and future pickleball addicts!

A special thank you to my loving husband, Todd. For without his help, encouragement, and pickleball knowledge, this book would not have been written.

Additionally, thank you to my mom who started Todd and me on this pickleball journey when she introduced me to the sport!

TABLE OF
CONTENTS

Introduction

Dubbed the "fastest growing sport in America," the growth of pickleball is absolutely exploding — and for good reason. The game provides many benefits and is enjoyed by people of all ages and backgrounds!

It's fun. It's competitive. It's social. It's active. It's easy to learn. It reduces stress and it can create healthy habits in those that play. Many admit to having a pickleball addiction. In fact, the hashtag, #PickleballisLife, is frequently used on social networks.

There are countless stories of how pickleball has positively impacted players' lives. While the benefits are certainly clear, they are also temporal. While pickleball can undoubtedly help in many areas of your life – **there's only one thing that can help in ALL areas of your life and beyond – and that is having a personal relationship with Jesus Christ.** *He* is life and *He* is the most important thing!

My husband, Todd, and I, absolutely love pickleball. Todd is a pickleball instructor and, together, we are blessed to have a pickleball business – one that we've had for the last several years. We are excited to see pickleball grow into such a popular sport.

With the growth of the sport skyrocketing – and locally, with the people that we personally meet on the courts – I started to get nudged by God. He would show me players who love the sport and are seemingly addicted to it – yet are still missing something. That something is Him.

God laid the idea for this book on my heart. I definitely didn't feel qualified to write a devotional book. Actually, I put it off for a while. However, between God continuing to tug at my heart and my husband encouraging me to start writing it, this book became a reality.

I pray this book will plant a seed in your heart and/or draw you closer to God. If you don't know Christ as your personal Savior, I pray that you will ultimately make a decision to follow Him. For those who already know Him, I pray this book can be used as a resource in your pickleball club or church group.

Oh, and, by the way – in addition to providing a framework for drawing closer to God – this book will, secondarily, provide tips and strategies to improve your pickleball game.

What's in This Book

This book was written to give you a simple daily devotional for 31 days.

Each of the 31 days consists of the following:

- Topic or Theme for the day
- Bible verse(s) related to that topic
- Short commentary on the verses/topic
- Pickleball tip
- Questions or challenges to ponder
- An area for you to write down some goals (spiritual or pickleball) as it relates to the daily topic
- An area to write out a prayer related to the daily topic

Also included in the book are 30 bonus pickleball strategies, a pickleball skills checklist, a page about prayer, and, most importantly, a page about salvation.

For additional pickleball tips and strategies, visit our website at:

www.PickleballMAX.com

"God calls us to use our abilities to our greatest potential for His glory, and that includes whenever we step on the field [court]. It's not to beat the guy next to you; it's to recognize it as an opportunity from God to reveal His glory."

Case Keenum
— NFL Quarterback

31 DAYS OF
DEVOTIONALS

Fear Not

Fear (**F**alse **E**vidence **A**ppearing **R**eal) can plague every area of our lives, even in pickleball. Playing at a new venue for the first time, or playing in a tournament can stir up fear and anxiety. However, God's Word says not to fear because He is with you. He's got it when it comes to any situation. Focus on Him. He will see you through.

... Fear not, for I have redeemed you; I have called you by name, you are mine. When you pass through the waters, I will be with you...Because you are precious in my eyes, and honored, and I love you...

— ISAIAH 43:1,2,4 (ESV)

For the Spirit God gave us does not make us timid, but gives us power, love and self-discipline.

— 2 TIMOTHY 1:7 (NIV)

PICKLEBALL TIP

Do not be overly anxious or nervous when playing a team for the first time. Stick to your game plan. Do what you do well. Then, make in-game adjustments as needed. You have prepared for this moment. You got this!

Are there areas in pickleball in which you are fearful?

....

....

Do your fears hold you back or cost you when it comes to health and happiness? How can you overcome your fear with God's help?

....

....

PRAYER

Dear Lord...
....

....

In Jesus Name, Amen.
....

SET SOME GOALS ◀◀

....

....

....

Jesus Gives Life

In pickleball, there are many different plans/strategies that can be implemented to achieve victory — which side of the court will you and your partner play on, will you dink or drive the shot, will you serve deep or short, will you hit to your opponent's forehand or backhand, etc?

Similarly, some people believe there may be many different ways to get to heaven. However, the Bible clearly states that **there is only ONE way — believing in Jesus Christ**. He is the only way. We are saved by GRACE! There is no Plan B or a different strategy that can be implemented at the end of one's life to get to heaven. You are heaven-bound only by receiving God's free gift of salvation.

Jesus answered, "I am the way and the truth and the life. No one comes to the Father except through me."

— JOHN 14:6 (NIV)

For God so loved the world that he gave his one and only Son, that whoever believes in him shall not perish but have eternal life.

— JOHN 3:16 (NIV)

PICKLEBALL TIP

When playing competitively, always have a Plan A, a Plan B (and a Plan C). Be willing to make in-game adjustments as the game or opponents dictate.

How do you determine which strategy you will implement against a specific opponent?

....

....

Do you know without a shadow of a doubt that you're going to heaven when you die? If not, why not accept God's gift of salvation today? *(See salvation prayer at the end of this book)*

....

PRAYER

Dear Lord.....

....

In Jesus Name, Amen.

....

SET SOME GOALS ◀◀

....

....

....

God's Word

In pickleball, we prepare for our next match by studying videos, watching professional matches, and seeking advice from instructors/influencers about how to play and win.

In life, however, there is only one thing we need in order to train and be fully equipped — the Bible. God gave us His Word to equip us and speak to us. The Bible is sharper than any double-edged sword. It's alive and active. If you don't do it already, start reading it today. You'll be glad you did!

All Scripture is breathed out by God and profitable for teaching, for reproof, for correction, and for training in righteousness, that the man of God may be complete, equipped for every good work.

— 2 TIMOTHY 3:16-17 (ESV)

For the word of God is alive and active. Sharper than any double-edged sword, it penetrates even to dividing soul and spirit, joints and marrow; it judges the thoughts and attitudes of the heart.

— HEBREWS 4:12 (NIV)

PICKLEBALL TIP

Train your shots. Drill with a partner or against the wall. Use a ball machine. Take a lesson from a qualified instructor. Learn proper technique and strategy.

POINTS TO PONDER

Which instructional pickleball videos do you watch? Which pickleball podcasts do you listen to?

....

....

Do you take time to read God's Word — the Bible? If you don't already, when can you take time to read it during the day?

....

....

PRAYER

Dear Lord...
....

....

In Jesus Name, Amen.
....

SET SOME GOALS ◀◀

....

....

....

Seek Christ First

We all know pickleball is a great game for so many reasons! It's easy to get addicted and want to play all of the time. When not on the court, you might constantly think about it or watch every video you can find. While all of that is good, there's more to life than pickleball. It shouldn't be anyone's #1 priority.

As a Christian, God should be the top priority. We need to prioritize time with Him in prayer and reading His Word. **Prioritize pray over play!**

But seek first his kingdom and his righteousness, and all these things will be given to you as well.

— MATTHEW 6:33 (NIV)

But blessed is the one who trusts in the Lord, whose confidence is in him.

— JEREMIAH 17:7 (NIV)

PICKLEBALL TIP

Consider videoing yourself on the practice court. Then objectively review the video to identify areas for improvement. It will undoubtedly make you a better pickleball player.

How many hours a week do you play pickleball?

....

....

How many hours a week do you spend praying, praising, or reading the Bible? Are you spending enough quality time with God?

....

....

PRAYER

Dear Lord...
....

....

In Jesus Name, Amen.
....

SET SOME GOALS ◀◀

....

....

....

Armor of God

God has given those who believe in Him powerful weaponry for everyday life. For example, we should put His armor *(see verses below)* on every day so it will protect us from satan's schemes and attacks. Are you consistently putting it on?

Similar to how we need God's armor for defending against attacks in our daily lives, there are things we can do in pickleball daily to perform at our highest level and prepare us for "battle." Drilling, mental training, and taking care of our bodies are good habits to exhibit on a regular basis.

Therefore put on the full armor of God, so that when the day of evil comes, you may be able to stand your ground, and after you have done everything, to stand. Stand firm then, with the belt of truth buckled around your waist, with the breastplate of righteousness in place, and with your feet fitted with the readiness that comes from the gospel of peace. In addition to all this, take up the shield of faith, with which you can extinguish all the flaming arrows of the evil one. Take the helmet of salvation and the sword of the Spirit, which is the word of God.

— EPHESIANS 6: 13-17 (NIV)

PICKLEBALL TIP

Add skinny singles to your drill routine. Skinny singles closely mimics the variety of shots that would be executed in a "real" game.

What are you consistently doing to prepare for pickleball game play?

....

....

Why do these verses about God's armor emphasize standing instead of sitting or walking?

....

....

PRAYER

Dear Lord.....

....

In Jesus Name, Amen.
....

SET SOME GOALS ◀◀

....

....

....

Fruit of the Spirit

The fruit of the Spirit includes virtuous characteristics that become more and more evident in our lives as we follow God's way. They grow in our lives just as fruit grows on a tree that is properly cared for.

In pickleball, our improved skills become more and more evident to our opponents as we practice and grow as a player. We need to properly care for all facets of our game.

But the fruit of the Spirit is love, joy, peace, patience, kindness, goodness, faithfulness, gentleness, self-control; against such things there is no law.

— GALATIANS 5: 22-23 (ESV)

For the entire law is fulfilled in keeping this one command: "Love your neighbor as yourself."

— GALATIANS 5:14 (NIV)

PICKLEBALL TIP

Learn to hit — by practice and drilling — unattackable dinks and drops, penetrating forehand and backhand drives, and a deep serve that puts the receiving team on the defensive. Don't forget to add roll volleys, resets, and an effective return-of-serve to your repotoire.

What skills do you need to work on as a pickleball player to grow your game?

....

....

Are you demonstrating the fruits of the Spirit in your daily life? If not, what are some things that might be holding you back from the fruit God wants to grow in your life?

....

....

PRAYER

Dear Lord...
....

....

In Jesus Name, Amen.
....

SET SOME GOALS ◀◀

....

....

....

Encourage Others

Life can be hard. It can even be hard on the court, especially after you make a bevy of unforced errors. God's Word says we should encourage others. The definition of encourage is "to inspire with courage, spirit, or confidence."

Receiving encouragement can lift someone's spirits whether it's on or off the court. Encouragement can boost a person's mindset and even get them to play better during a game.

Therefore encourage one another and build one another up...

— 1 THESSALONIANS 5:11a (ESV)

PICKLEBALL TIP

Paddle tap with your partner after a good shot and between rallies. It's a gesture of encouragement. It's a way of communicating with each other without actually saying, "Let's go," or "We got this."

What are some things you can do to encourage others on the court?

....

....

Think back to a time when you needed encouragement. What did someone do to encourage you?

....

....

PRAYER

Dear Lord...
....

....

In Jesus Name, Amen.
....

SET SOME GOALS ◄◄

....

....

....

Two are Better Than One

We shouldn't do life alone. We can learn from each other's counsel and experiences. We can also help each other out in times of need.

This rings true when playing doubles in pickleball. You and your partner can strategize together and leverage each other's skills and abilities to become a powerhouse team.

Two people are better off than one, for they can help each other succeed. If one person falls, the other can reach out and help. But someone who falls alone is in real trouble.

— ECCLESIASTES 4:9-10 (NLT)

PICKLEBALL TIP

Talk to your partner. Communicate by calling "mine" or "yours." Remember, you're a team!

POINTS TO PONDER

How can you help your doubles partner when you're on the court?

....

....

What can you do to help someone who is in need?

....

....

PRAYER

Dear Lord.....

....

In Jesus Name, Amen.

....

SET SOME GOALS ◀◀

....

....

....

Iron Sharpens Iron

Years ago, my husband wrote a blog post on PickleballMAX about being a cardboard cutout. He was growing frustrated by players who were not hitting him the ball. Perhaps they were intimidated because he was one of the better players in the area at the time. However, his opponents had a great opportunity if they would have hit the ball to him. Their game would have started to improve playing against a better player.

Don't miss the opportunity to improve your game if you're playing against a better player. As God's Word says, "Iron sharpens iron."

In life, it's important to surround yourself with others who can motivate you and encourage you to be your best. God has gifted each one of us. We can learn from each other.

As iron sharpens iron, so one person sharpens another.

— PROVERBS 27:17 (NIV)

PICKLEBALL TIP

If the opportunity arises to play against a better player, make an effort to hit them the ball. By doing so, you will get a better understanding of your strengths and weaknesses, which will only help to improve your own game — even if it means losing a recreational game here or there.

When was the last time you challenged yourself by hitting the ball to the better player without caring if you won or lost?

....

....

Have you surrounded yourself with people who can sharpen you?

....

....

PRAYER

Dear Lord... ....

....

In Jesus Name, Amen.
....

SET SOME GOALS ◀◀

....

....

....

Be Humble

We've all heard the saying — "pride comes before a fall". Have you ever played with or against someone who thought they were all that? Over time they get a reputation and eventually, nobody wants to play with them. No matter how good we are, it's important to stay humble in victory and gracious in defeat.

That rings true in daily life as well. Humility will take you farther in life. Wisdom will come from listening to others. There's no need to be boastful.

For all those who exalt themselves will be humbled, and those who humble themselves will be exalted.

— LUKE 14:11 (NIV)

When pride comes, then comes disgrace, but with humility comes wisdom.

— PROVERBS 11:2 (NIV)

PICKLEBALL TIP

Don't chest-bump or be excessive in the celebration when your opponent makes an error. The same goes for "spectators." Please don't clap or cheer when the opposing player misses an easy shot.

Think of the last time you were victorious. How did you react? Were you gracious or did you rub it in to the opposing team?

....

....

When God blesses you with success, do you become prideful, or do you give Him the glory?

....

....

PRAYER

Dear Lord...
....

....

In Jesus Name, Amen.
....

SET SOME GOALS ⟪

....

....

....

Don't Be Lazy

As a pickleball player, you're not lazy. You've gotten out of the chair and got onto the court. As a player, you're getting exercise, socialization, and hopefully improved health. Once on the court, you need to work hard in order to prosper or improve your game. Don't be like the lazy person who cuts corners by not drilling or practicing. Work hard and watch your game grow.

In addition to the verses below, there are so many great nuggets for life throughout the book of Proverbs. Take time to read through the book and apply the wisdom it imparts to your life.

Lazy people want much but get little, but those who work hard will prosper.

— PROVERBS 13:4 (NLT)

Lazy hands make for poverty, but diligent hands bring wealth.

— PROVERBS 10:4 (NIV)

PICKLEBALL TIP

Practice time needs to mimic the focus, intention and purpose of a "real game" — all while adding in a layer of mental pressure — pressure that you're sure to encounter in a "real" game. Do drills. Review video.

What are some things you can incorporate into your daily routine to improve your game?

....

....

Are there areas in your life where you are procrastinating? Do you feel like you could achieve more if you procrastinated less?

....

....

PRAYER

Dear Lord.....

....

In Jesus Name, Amen.
....

SET SOME GOALS ◀◀

....

....

....

Listen Up

Fortunately, there are those who have gone before you as a player. They might have been playing for years, or have learned from some of the pros. It's important to take advice from those players so you can up your game. If you want to improve, take lessons from an instructor and follow their advice.

The same is true in life. Heed the advice of someone who has already been there/done that. They might be able to save you from headaches on life's journey.

Listen to advice and accept instruction, that you may gain wisdom in the future.

— PROVERBS 19:20 (ESV)

The Lord will make you the head, not the tail. If you pay attention to the commands of the Lord your God that I give you this day and carefully follow them, you will always be at the top, never at the bottom.

— DEUTERONOMY 28:13 (NIV)

PICKLEBALL TIP

For some of the larger tournaments, clinics are frequently hosted at the tournament venue a few days before the tourney begins. Take advantage of the great instruction — sometimes even given by the pros!

Have you attended a pickleball clinic or taken a lesson? What did you learn?

....

....

Is there an area you're struggling with in your life? Is there someone honest and trustworthy you could ask for advice?

....

....

PRAYER

Dear Lord...
....

....

In Jesus Name, Amen.
....

SET SOME GOALS ◀◀

....

....

....

Your Treasure

In life, it's easy to get caught up in working hard to make more-and-more money. In pickleball, it's easy to get addicted to playing and collecting tournament medals. However, God's Word says the things you collect on earth are temporary. They can be stolen or destroyed. At the end of life, it's not about the podium results, medals, or your skill rating.

God's Word says we will be accountable for what we've done on earth. We will be rewarded in heaven. Take time to encourage someone. Share the Gospel with others. Invite someone to church. Those are the things that will matter in the end.

As fun as it is to collect tournament medals, they will, unfortunately, just fade away, or get lost in the dresser drawer. What you do to further God's kingdom on earth will last eternally.

> *Do not store up for yourselves treasures on earth, where moths and vermin destroy, and where thieves break in and steal. But store up for yourselves treasures in heaven, where moths and vermin do not destroy, and where thieves do not break in and steal. For where your treasure is, there your heart will be also.*
>
> **— MATTHEW 6:19-21 (NIV)**

> *Everyone who competes in the games goes into strict training. They do it to get a crown that will not last, but we do it to get a crown that will last forever.*
>
> **— 1 CORINTHIANS 9:25 (NIV)**

PICKLEBALL TIP

When your team is at the non-volley line and your opponents are deep in the court, keep them deep. You want to keep them away from the most strategic spot on the court.

How can you store up treasure in heaven as a pickleball player?

....

....

If you were given one million dollars, what would you do with it? (After reading Matthew 6:19-21)

....

....

PRAYER

Dear Lord...
....

....

In Jesus Name, Amen.
....

SET SOME GOALS

....

....

....

Give Thanks

Every day is a gift from God. He created this world that we can enjoy. Even if you have a bad day, you can wake up the next morning and thank God for another day to start over again.

If you're able to play pickleball, be grateful that there's a sport you can play, and one in which you can have fun doing so. Be thankful that you're healthy enough to play. Be happy for the new friendships you have as a result of pickleball. God is good and He loves you. Rejoice in that!

Give thanks to the Lord, for he is good; his love endures forever.

— PSALMS 118:1 (NIV)

This is the day that the Lord has made; let us rejoice and be glad in it.

— PSALMS 118:24 (ESV)

PICKLEBALL TIP

When warming up prior to hitting the courts, begin with some walking or light jogging to get your heart pumping. This raises your body temperature and readies your heart and lungs for exercising as well as warms your muscles.

How do you give thanks on a regular basis?

....

....

What are some of the reasons that you aren't as grateful as you should be?

....

....

Do you have a grateful jar or journal? Try writing down 1 thing you're grateful for every day.

PRAYER

Dear Lord......

....

In Jesus Name, Amen.
....

SET SOME GOALS ◀◀

....

....

....

Guard Your Tongue

There are many stories of players who get a partner or opponent who constantly gives advice on the court. Maybe they thought your serve should go deeper, or you should have hit a drop instead of a drive (and they let you know it). Everyone plays pickleball for a different reason. Some want to improve their game while others just want to exercise or socialize.

The Bible says we should guard our mouths. Even if you have a great tip to impart to another player, it's, no doubt, best to ask if they would like the advice before giving it. If they don't want the advice, keep it to yourself. You might just save yourself a friendship.

Those who guard their mouths and their tongues keep themselves from calamity.

— PROVERBS 21:23 (NIV)

PICKLEBALL TIP

Don't give unsolicited advice on the court. Although likely, helpful, it's rarely welcomed. Instead, wait until the match is over, and, privately, ask if they would like some feedback. They will, no doubt, be much more receptive to your offer.

POINTS TO PONDER

Do you give unsolicited advice on the court?

....

....

What are some actions you can take to control your tongue?

....

....

PRAYER

Dear Lord...
....

....

In Jesus Name, Amen.
....

SET SOME GOALS

....

....

....

Discernment

Today's world provides many distractions for our thoughts and time. Our job, family, friends, technology, hobbies, and health can zap our time. They can also become idols in our lives if we're constantly thinking about them. God warns us throughout His Word to keep ourselves from idols. We have to be careful not to misalign our priorities. God should be our top priority. We shouldn't take Him for granted. He is the truth in a world that can seem upside-down and chaotic.

The same holds true in pickleball. If you focus on it 24/7, you will get burned out. Don't become distracted by pickleball. That can keep you from what God has for you. Slow down and take time to listen to God. When you make Him your top priority and focus on His will, everything else will fall into place.

> *We know also that the Son of God has come and has given us understanding, so that we may know him who is true. And we are in him who is true by being in his Son Jesus Christ. He is the true God and eternal life. Dear children, keep yourselves from idols.*
>
> **— 1 JOHN 5:20-21**

PICKLEBALL TIP

When your team is at the NV line and your opponents are deep in the court, keep them deep. You want to keep them away from the most strategic spot on the court.

Have you been given bad advice in pickleball? How do you discern what's correct and what's not?

....

....

What do you think about when nothing else demands your attention?

....

....

PRAYER

Dear Lord.....

....

In Jesus Name, Amen.
....

SET SOME GOALS ◀◀

....

....

....

Be Strong & Courageous

Even though pickleball is a great sport, there are times we might get discouraged or afraid. Discouragement can come after a bad day on the court — losing all of your rec games after dominating the day before. Or you might be intimidated to play in your first tournament.

Isn't it comforting to know that the Lord is with us wherever we are? As a child of God, we don't need to be afraid or be discouraged. He will not abandon us. He will also strengthen us when we ask for it. Keep your mind fixed on Him.

This is my command—be strong and courageous! Do not be afraid or discouraged. For the Lord your God is with you wherever you go.

— JOSHUA 1:9 (NLT)

Do not be afraid or discouraged, for the Lord will personally go ahead of you. He will be with you; he will neither fail you nor abandon you.

— DEUTERONOMY 31:8 (NLT)

PICKLEBALL TIP

Change your mental mindset from "being afraid of losing" to "loving the battle." Then, train and practice this mindset.

POINTS TO PONDER

When you attend a tournament, will you approach your opponent timidly, or will you walk out on the court courageously? Will you pray for God's strength or just enter the court on your own accord?

....

....

Think of a time when you were discouraged on the court (or in life). How did you handle it? Did you pray and thank God that He is with you, or did you wallow in discouragement?

....

....

PRAYER

Dear Lord.....

....

In Jesus Name, Amen.
....

SET SOME GOALS ◀◀

....

....

....

Press On

After making needless unforced errors in the prior game, it's difficult to not dwell on it. Continuing to think about past errors takes your focus away from the next game. It takes mental toughness to forget about it and press on, but that's what God's Word says we need to do. Keep moving forward on the court and in life.

God has a purpose for your life. He doesn't want you to get stuck along the way. Keep pressing toward the goal He has given you.

Brothers and sisters, I do not consider myself yet to have taken hold of it. But one thing I do: Forgetting what is behind and straining toward what is ahead, I press on toward the goal to win the prize for which God has called me heavenward in Christ Jesus.

— PHILIPPIANS 3:13-14 (NIV)

PICKLEBALL TIP

Have a short-term memory. Forget about previous mistakes or points you should have won. Concentrate only on the next point.

POINTS TO PONDER

Is there an area in your life (or game) where you are stuck? What can you start doing to move forward?

....

....

Has God given you a specific purpose for your life? If you're not sure, ask Him to reveal it to you.

....

....

PRAYER

Dear Lord...
....

....

In Jesus Name, Amen.
....

SET SOME GOALS ◀◀

....

....

....

Keep the Faith

You might have been there. The score was 0-10-1. You and your partner were ready to finish the current game and start a new one. However, you didn't give up. You served and racked up 6 straight points. With a score of 6-10-2, your partner was able to rack up 2 additional points. You hustled and were on a roll! The serve went to the other team, then you held them at 10. You were able to close out the game with a few more points. It was an amazing comeback! You didn't give up.

God's Word says not to give up. He encourages us to keep the faith and finish the race. In life, this means living it all the way to the end. Be a Christlike example for others. Share Christ. No matter what the age, we can all be used by God to impact others.

I have fought the good fight, I have finished the race, I have kept the faith.

— 2 TIMOTHY 4:7 (NIV)

But as for you, be strong and do not give up, for your work will be rewarded.

— 2 CHRONICLES 15:7 (NIV)

PICKLEBALL TIP

Grind for every point. Sometimes matches are decided by getting just one more ball back!

Think back to a time when you were behind by several points in a game. Did you give up and lose, or did you persevere until the end (whether you won or not)?

....

....

What are some reasons why you might give up? How can you overcome them with God's help?

....

....

PRAYER

Dear Lord...
....

....

In Jesus Name, Amen.
....

SET SOME GOALS ≪

....

....

....

When Trials Come

Nobody wants to face trials. However, trials are inevitable. We all face them at some point in our lives. The Bible says that trials are used to produce perseverance. While not fun at the time, if you look at a trial after going through it, you can typically learn something from it to apply to your life.

In pickleball, it can be hard to lose a game, especially if you lose several in a row. You might be stuck in a rut, or have the serving yips. Maybe you've had to take time off the court due to an injury. Whichever the case, you can persevere and learn something from those instances and apply it to future games. Trials on the court can ultimately be a good thing as they can provide opportunities for improvement.

Consider it pure joy, my brothers and sisters, whenever you face trials of many kinds, because you know that the testing of your faith produces perseverance.

— JAMES 1: 2-3 (NIV)

PICKLEBALL TIP

Learn from your defeats. What could you have done better? Work on these shortcomings. Improvement will then come quickly.

POINTS TO PONDER

Have you ever encountered a setback in pickleball? How did you handle it?

....

....

Did you use your setback for an opportunity to grow in Christ, or did you wallow in self pity?

....

....

PRAYER

Dear Lord.....

....

In Jesus Name, Amen.

....

SET SOME GOALS ≪

....

....

....

Taking time to practice every day isn't always fun, but if you want to grow as a player, it's necessary. Doing repetitive drills with a partner or ball machine — while boring to most — will create muscle-memory so you can execute at a high level during a game.

God's Word addresses the concept of discipline. While discipline isn't pleasant at the time, it leads to success for those who have put in the time. Put in the time and effort and see where it takes you.

> *No discipline seems pleasant at the time, but painful. Later on, however, it produces a harvest of righteousness and peace for those who have been trained by it.*
>
> **— HEBREWS 12: 11 (NIV)**

PICKLEBALL TIP

Incorporate targets into your practice routine and drill your shots repetitively. With instant feedback, you will then be able to tweak the mechanics of the shot as you rally or drill.

POINTS TO PONDER

Do you take time to drill? What are some drills you can add to your practice routine?

....

....

Are you disciplined in your spiritual life?

....

....

PRAYER

Dear Lord...
....

....

In Jesus Name, Amen.
....

SET SOME GOALS

....

....

....

Be Selfless

Pickleball has benefited over the years with players giving back to the sport. Many have wanted to grow it – not out of selfish ambition – but as a way to share something great with others. They have become ambassadors, played with newer players, volunteered at tournaments, etc. You are probably playing pickleball as a result of someone who took the time to introduce you to the sport.

God's Word says we should put others before ourselves. This rings true in life as well as in pickleball. Just think what the world would be like if everyone exhibited selflessness.

Do nothing out of selfish ambition or vain conceit. Rather, in humility value others above yourselves, not looking to your own interests but each of you to the interests of the others.

— PHILIPPIANS 2:3-4 (NIV)

PICKLEBALL TIP

If you are obviously the strongest person in your foursome, tone down the competitiveness and hit your opponents' balls that they can return. Work on a new skill – perhaps it's a great time for work on that third shot drop shot. This will be a benefit to both of you.

POINTS TO PONDER

Are you becoming an ambassador by introducing new people to pickleball? Do you volunteer at tournaments?

....

....

What does it mean to value others above yourself? When was the last time you put someone before yourself?

....

....

PRAYER

Dear Lord.....

....

In Jesus Name, Amen.
....

SET SOME GOALS ◄◄

....

....

....

Obedience

Living a Godly life isn't a cakewalk. You're going to have rough days, just like everyone else. The difference is you have someone you can go to with your problems. He will take your burdens and He will guide you through life if you trust in Him.

Walking in obedience to Christ takes reading the Bible and spending time in prayer so you will know what He wants you to do. God's counsel can save you from making poor decisions. That can even ring true on the court.

Obey God's commands. Take them to heart and practice them.

Walk in obedience to all that the Lord your God has commanded you, so that you may live and prosper and prolong your days in the land that you will possess.

— DEUTERONOMY 5:33 (NIV)

PICKLEBALL TIP

Footwork – Slide while leading with your outside leg when dinking or volleying at the NVZ if possible. Doing so will help you stay square to your opponent and the oncoming ball.

Do you give your opponent the benefit of doubt on line calls if you're not sure?

....

....

Why does God want us to obey His commands? When was the last time you consulted with God before making a decision?

....

....

PRAYER

Dear Lord.....

....

In Jesus Name, Amen.
....

SET SOME GOALS ◀◀

....

....

....

Grow

A baby starts off by drinking milk. Liquids or soft foods are all that they can handle. However, as a child grows and develops, they can start adding new foods to their diet.

Similar to a baby, initially a new Christian takes in milk (reading God's Word). As they grow, so will their faith and wisdom.

Dinking is inarguably pickleball's initial and most important skill to learn and master. As you improve, work on other fundamentals, including serves, volleys, drops, and drives. Then, incorporate other shots that you don't hit as often, such as an ATP or scorpion.

Both in life and on the pickleball court, we can build upon experiences in order to grow.

I gave you milk, not solid food, for you were not yet ready for it. Indeed, you are still not ready.

— 1 CORINTHIANS 3:2 (NIV)

PICKLEBALL TIP

With all four players positioned at their own non-volley lines, dinking the ball into your opponent's non-volley zone forces your opponent to "hit up" on their next shot. It's, arguably, the most important shot in pickleball.

POINTS TO PONDER

Has there been a time in your life or on the court where you tried to do something that would have been better if you would have waited and mastered a more basic skill first?

....

....

What are some things you can do to mature or grow in your relationship with Christ?

....

....

PRAYER

Dear Lord......

....

....*In Jesus Name, Amen.*

SET SOME GOALS ◀◀

....

....

....

Be on Guard

In life, we need to be on guard as satan roams around like a lion seeking those whom he can devour. We want to be grounded in our faith so we can withstand these attacks.

This concept is similar to that of being in a good ready position on the court. You want to be in a good position so you can easily combat the shots your opponent hits at you. Bending your knees with your feet shoulder-width apart puts you in a solid stance so you can block a shot or return it with your forehand or backhand. Holding the paddle in front of your body is like holding the breastplate of God's armor. It blocks a shot from your opponent on the court. In life, the breastplate blocks a firey shot that satan uses to attack you.

On the court and in life, stand on guard and be courageous. You are a child of God!

Be on your guard; stand firm in the faith; be courageous; be strong.

— 1 CORINTHIANS 16:13 (NIV)

PICKLEBALL TIP

Prior to your opponent hitting their shot, be in the ready position – with feet shoulder-width apart, knees slightly bent, weight on the balls of your feet and paddle in front of your body.

POINTS TO PONDER

Are you in a balanced ready position on the court to combat shots from your opponent?

....

....

Did you know that satan wants to deceive, distract and destroy you? What precautions are you taking to combat satan's attacks?

....

....

PRAYER

Dear Lord...
....

....

In Jesus Name, Amen.
....

SET SOME GOALS ◀◀

....

....

....

Endurance & Perseverance

Perseverance is a great characteristic to perfect. You must have the endurance to persevere. Whether in life or pickleball, you will have hindrances that come at you and try to stop you or throw you off course. It takes perseverance and endurance to move forward. God has a plan for your life and He will see you through if you let Him. Don't get hung up along the way.

On the court, moving from the baseline to the most strategic area on the court (Non-Volley Zone) takes perseverance. Your opponent might keep hitting drives in an attempt to keep you pinned to the baseline. But you need to keep hitting drop shots and resets to move forward. It might take a few shots, but you can make it.

being strengthened with all power according to his glorious might so that you may have great endurance and patience,

— COLOSSIANS 1:11 (NIV)

Therefore, since we are surrounded by such a great cloud of witnesses, let us throw off everything that hinders and the sin that so easily entangles. And let us run with perseverance the race marked out for us,

— HEBREWS 12:1 (NIV)

PICKLEBALL TIP

Don't worry if you cannot make it all the way from the baseline to the kitchen line before your opponent is ready to strike the ball. Depending on your speed and quickness, it may take you a couple of shots to get all the way in. That's perfectly fine. Just remember to split step!

Remember back to a time when you felt stuck in life or on the court. What helped you move forward?

....

....

What are some ways in which you can improve your endurance (on and off the court)?

....

....

PRAYER

Dear Lord.....

....

In Jesus Name, Amen.
....

SET SOME GOALS ◄◄

....

....

....

Live in Harmony

The word pride and/or proud is mentioned over 100 times in the Bible, so this characteristic is very important to God. He warns of it throughout His Word. He wants us to keep a humble attitude in life and live in harmony with others. This also applies to the pickleball court. Even though you might be a great player or even a professional player, it's important to keep your attitude in check. Be a gracious winner.

Play with those who are at a lower rank than you from time to time. All of us have been there — starting out as a 2.0 or 3.0 player when we first picked up a paddle. I'm sure you can remember back to when a higher-level player invested their time in you. It makes a huge impact and it helps grow the sport.

Live in harmony with one another. Do not be proud, but be willing to associate with people of low position.
Do not be conceited.

— ROMANS 12:16 (NIV)

PICKLEBALL TIP

Remember your roots. Play with "lower" level players from time-to-time. They will appreciate and respect you.

Does your pickleball club have a mentorship program? If not, could you start one?

....

....

Why is it important to live in harmony with others? Do you exhibit humility or are you prideful?

....

....

PRAYER

Dear Lord...
....

....

In Jesus Name, Amen.
....

SET SOME GOALS ◄◄

....

....

....

Judge Correctly

Pickleball is such a great sport in that all ages can play. What used to be a sport for seniors has transformed over the years to be a sport for the younger generation as well. Have you ever arrived at the court and were paired with a senior couple? You thought it was going to be easy to beat them, but in the end, the seniors came away victorious! Likewise, have you looked at a younger player and thought there's no way they could be on the board of your pickleball club? They don't have enough experience, or so you thought. However, they turn out to be a great addition to the board.

There are many verses in God's Word that say we shouldn't judge someone just by their looks. God judges the heart. Next time you're on the court, be sure to give everyone a chance by playing with them. Don't write them off as soon as you see them.

> *Don't let anyone look down on you because you are young, but set an example for the believers in speech, in conduct, in love, in faith and in purity.*
>
> **— 1 TIMOTHY 4: 12 (NIV)**

> *Stop judging by mere appearances, but instead judge correctly.*
>
> **— JOHN 7:24 (NIV)**

PICKLEBALL TIP

Be an example to others on the pickleball court. Offer helpful advice if/when asked. Consider being a mentor, or starting a mentorship program at your club. "Newbies" will appreciate your willingness to help.

Have you decided not to play with someone based on their age, or what they're wearing? How can you start including others in games?

....

....

If you're young, how does 1 Timothy 4:12 say you can serve as an example?

....

....

PRAYER

Dear Lord......

....

In Jesus Name, Amen.
....

SET SOME GOALS ≪

....

....

....

Revenge Not

I imagine we've all been there. Either we've played against someone who is hot-tempered and revengeful on the court, or we've heard of it happening to someone else. Nobody likes to play with someone who stirs up conflict or becomes revengeful.

If your opponent accidentally "tattooed" you, or you lost the game because of a bad line call, don't try to seek revenge or throw a fit on the court. Go out in the next game and try to win fair-and-square. Sometimes not saying anything can speak louder than words.

Do not seek revenge or bear a grudge against anyone among your people, but love your neighbor as yourself. I am the Lord.

— LEVITICUS 19:18 (NIV)

A hot-tempered person stirs up conflict, but the one who is patient calms a quarrel.

— PROVERBS 15:18 (NIV)

PICKLEBALL TIP

If your opponents are predictably targeting your [weaker] partner, consider poaching from time-to-time to disrupt and catch your opponents off guard.

Was there ever a time when you lost it on the court? Did you try to seek revenge? Pray for God's forgiveness and apologize to the person towards whom your anger was directed.

....

....

What does it mean to love your neighbor as yourself?

....

....

PRAYER

Dear Lord...
....

....

In Jesus Name, Amen.
....

SET SOME GOALS ◄◄

....

....

....

Delight in the Lord

In life, it's a good practice to always consult with God. He wants to be involved in your life. Trust in Him and seek Him with your plans. As you're in His Word and listening to Him in prayer, your desires will begin to align with His will. He will give you the desires of your heart.

This can also be true in pickleball. Make Him a top priority in your life. He can open up different avenues, or create new relationships for you in the sport. Take your desires to Him and see what He will do.

Take delight in the Lord, and he will give you the desires of your heart.

— PSALMS 37:4 (NIV)

Commit to the Lord whatever you do, and he will establish your plans.

— PROVERBS 16:3 (NIV)

PICKLEBALL TIP

If the ball at the point of contact is above the net, a drive may be the best shot. If the ball is at or below net level, however, a "drop" is likely the better decision.

POINTS TO PONDER

Are you taking the time to build new relationships with other players, or are you just interested in winning a game?

....

....

What are some things you can start doing to take delight in the Lord?

....

....

PRAYER

Dear Lord...
....

....

In Jesus Name, Amen.
....

SET SOME GOALS ◀◀

....

....

....

Hope

Have you ever experienced an injury, or had to take an extended time away from pickleball? After months away from the court, you might be concerned about returning since it will take you time to get up to speed. The people you used to play with have advanced in their rankings while you were away.

Put your hope in the Lord. He will renew your strength. What looks impossible can be made possible through Him. Maybe when you return, it only takes you a couple of weeks to get back to where you were as a player. Then with practice and gameplay, you're quickly able to move up a rank to rejoin your friends. If you aren't able to rejoin your friends, see it as an opportunity to make new friends. God will put you right in the place that you should be. Maybe there's someone He wants you to impact. Wherever you play, you can soar because of Christ.

but those who hope in the Lord will renew their strength. They will soar on wings like eagles; they will run and not grow weary, they will walk and not be faint.

— ISAIAH 40:31 (NIV)

Jesus looked at them and said, "With man this is impossible, but with God all things are possible."

— MATTHEW 19:26 (NIV)

PICKLEBALL TIP

When retrieving a lob, attempt to hit your shot into your opponent's Non-Volley Zone – and then work your way back to your own Non-Volley Zone. *Remember:* Do not backpedal when going back to retrieve the lob.

Have you experienced an injury that kept you off of the court? How did you handle it? What did you learn during that time?

....

....

When problems come, where do you look for strength? Do you look to others, or do you look to a great God who will help you?

....

....

PRAYER

Dear Lord...
....

....

In Jesus Name, Amen.
....

SET SOME GOALS ◀◀

....

....

....

"We often can't see what God is doing in our lives, but God sees the whole picture and His plan for us clearly."

Tony Dungy
— NFL Coach

BONUS
CONTENT

The Gift of Salvation

Salvation is a free gift. God loves all of us so much that He sent His Son, Jesus, into this world as a sacrifice. Jesus took on our sins, died on the cross, and was resurrected so that those who believe can have eternal life with Him in heaven.

Pickleball is a great sport, but there's more to life than pickleball. Accepting God's gift of salvation not only gives us eternal life but also gives us access to God in our daily lives. Being God's child and living for His purpose IS life! I invite you to read through the following verses and if you truly believe in what the Bible says, accept God's gift of salvation.

for all have sinned and fall short of the glory of God,

— Romans 3:23 (NIV)

Accept that all have sinned (you are a sinner).

For the wages of sin is death, but the gift of God is eternal life in Christ Jesus our Lord.

— Romans 6:23 (NIV)

Believe that God has given you the gift of eternal life through Jesus' death.

But God demonstrates his own love for us in this: While we were still sinners, Christ died for us.

— Romans 5:8 (NIV)

Confess that Jesus is Lord, He died for your sins and rose again.

If you declare with your mouth, "Jesus is Lord," and believe in your heart that God raised him from the dead, you will be saved. For it is with your heart that you believe and are justified, and it is with your mouth that you profess your faith and are saved.

— Romans 10:9-10 (NIV)

for, "Everyone who calls on the name of the Lord will be saved."

— Romans 10:13 (NIV)

For it is by grace you have been saved, through faith—and this is not from yourselves, it is the gift of God — not by works, so that no one can boast.

— Ephesians 2:8-9 (NIV)

Yet to all who did receive him, to those who believed in his name, he gave the right to become children of God—

— John 1:12 (NIV)

Prayer for Salvation

Dear Lord,

I know I'm a sinner. I believe that you died to take away my sins, and then rose from the grave. Please forgive me of my sins. I trust you as my Savior. Thank you for your gift of salvation and for the eternal life I now have through you.

In Jesus name, Amen.

Welcome to God's family! This is the best decision anyone can make! You now know that when you die, you will be in Heaven with God. You also now have the Holy Spirit to guide you on earth for the rest of your life.

I encourage you to find a local Bible-believing church to attend so you can learn more about being a new life in Christ.

Prayer is Powerful

Prayer is our communication with God. As a child of God, we have the privilege of talking directly to our Father in heaven.

We should pray in all situations. Whether you are hurting, thankful, tempted, making a decision, discerning His will, or needing forgiveness, God is there to take your burdens and see you through. The Bible says we need to pray without ceasing (1 Thes 5:17). God wants to have a relationship with us. He will also speak to us if we take the time to listen.

Jesus gives us an example of how we should pray:

"This, then, is how you should pray:
"'Our Father in heaven, hallowed be your name,
your kingdom come, your will be done, on earth as it is in heaven.
Give us today our daily bread.
And forgive us our debts, as we also have forgiven our debtors.
And lead us not into temptation, but deliver us from the evil one.

— Matthew 6:9-13 NIV

As you read and understand the Bible, you can begin to pray God's words. The Bible says that His words will not return void:

so shall my word be that goes out from my mouth; it shall not return to me
empty, but it shall accomplish that which I purpose, and shall succeed in
the thing for which I sent it.

— Isaiah 55:11 (ESV)

The **Acts acronym** can be helpful to keep in mind when praying.

Adoration
   Confession
      Thanksgiving
         Supplication

No matter how you pray,
the important thing is you do it!

BONUS
PICKLEBALL
CONTENT

Pickleball Technique Checklist

DINKS

- ☐ Position Yourself 1-2 Inches Behind the Non-Volley Line
- ☐ Soft, Relaxed Grip
- ☐ Virtually No Backswing
- ☐ Bend the Knees / Stay Low
- ☐ Make Contact in Front of Body
- ☐ Lifting Motion (Low-to-High)
- ☐ Short, Abbreviated Follow Thru
- ☐ Comfortable Margin for Error Over Net

DROP SHOTS (3RD SHOT)

- ☐ Bend the Knees / Stay Low
- ☐ Shift your Weight to Front Foot
- ☐ Make Contact in Front of Body
- ☐ Lifting Motion (Low-to-High)
- ☐ Accelerate Thru the Shot
- ☐ Keep the Head Down
- ☐ Follow Thru (Little More than a Dink)
- ☐ Comfortable Margin for Error Over Net

DRIVES (GROUND STROKES)

- ☐ Shoulder Turn
- ☐ Paddle Back Early
- ☐ Weight Transfer to Your Front Foot
- ☐ Make Contact in Front of Body
- ☐ Low-to-High Swing Path
- ☐ Follow Thru
- ☐ Good Depth

VOLLEYS (PUNCH)

- ☐ Feet Shoulder-Width Apart
- ☐ Shoulders/Chest Square to Net
- ☐ Knees Slightly Bent
- ☐ Make Contact in Front of Body
- ☐ Extend Arm Forward from Elbow
- ☐ Paddle Face Should be Slightly Open
- ☐ Hit to Opponents' Feet or to a Gap

Bonus Pickleball Strategies

1. Hitting a drop shot cross-court is the "safer" shot (greater margin for error) because the target area is larger when you hit diagonally. It's all geometry!

2. Hit the ball at your opponents' feet – forcing them to hit up on the ball. By doing so, they will be unable to attack the ball.

3. The continental grip is recommended for volleys (both forehand & backhand) because it provides a relatively strong position on both sides. That is advantageous because there is little time to change grips when volleying.

4. Find and exploit your opponents' weaknesses.

5. Use your opponent's speed & quickness against them by hitting behind them – particularly effective when playing singles!

6. When returning serve, return it deep and get to the non-volley line. Points are more easily won at the net.

7. In singles, the serve should generally be executed near the centerline so that the server can effectively cover both sides of the court when the serve is returned.

8. When positioned at the non-volley line, make sure you are only an inch or two away from the line. It will reduce angles for your opponent and make it harder for them to hit the ball at your feet.

9. Don't be afraid to give yourself some margin for error over the net when executing dinks and drops. Make sure, however, that you still land the ball in the Non-Volley Zone – forcing your opponents to hit up.

10. For "routine" dinks – those that don't require much, if any, lateral or forward movement – it's unnecessary (and inefficient) to "step into" the ball (and into the Non-Volley Zone) to hit the ball.

11. Hitting a drop shot is an excellent shot selection any time you and your partner are not at the non-volley line, but your opponents are.

12   Patience — Stay patient when at the Non-Volley Zone and wait for a ball that you can hit with a descending blow.

13   Serving the ball deep in your opponent's court makes their return more difficult — and it also makes it more challenging for them to get to their own kitchen line after the return-of-serve.

14   A softer, higher, deeper return of serve may be the better strategic decision so that you're better able (have more time) to get to the non-volley line.

15   Hitting an offensive lob will drive your opponents off the non-volley line and, if executed well, will put you and your partner in a rally-winning position with you up and your opponents back in the court.

16   When the ball is near your partner's sideline and directly in front of your partner you will want to cover the middle while your partner covers their line.

17   The 2-handed backhand can be effectively used at any time – but particularly when you want additional power and/or stability – and you have adequate time in which to execute the shot.

18   An effective time to execute the roll volley is when you and your partner are positioned at the Non-Volley Line and your opponents are back and you want to keep them pinned to the baseline.

19   When the ball is near the middle of the court on your opponent's side, both you and your partner should shade to the middle.

20   When you see a pickleball player "wind up," take an exaggerated back-swing and try to hit a low ball hard, the chances of that ball going out is very high – especially if the ball was hit without topspin.

21   Regardless of where your opponent is positioned on the court, an important strategic rule of thumb is to hit the ball at your opponent's feet.

22 The middle of the court, generally speaking, is the area of the court that is the easiest for one to execute their shots. Therefore, shade to the middle to take away your opponent's easiest shot.

23 For those dinks that require a bit of lateral movement to return them, keep your body square to the court and slide along the line (just behind the line) until you are able to contact the ball comfortably in front of your body.

24 Arrive at the tournament courts early to check-in, get your court assignment and warm up. Make sure you stretch, practice your dinks, volleys, drives and serves and get your heart-rate elevated — perhaps with a game of skinny singles with your partner. You'll likely only get a 5-minute warm-up once your match is called.

25 To maintain balance, don't forget to split step as you transition from the baseline to the non-volley line.

26 Consider implementing a "stacking" strategy if one player on your team is right-handed and the other is left-handed. It will allow both players to hit shots down the middle with their forehand – presumably both players' stronger sides.

27 When playing singles, take all the possible angles your opponent can hit, and stand directly in the middle of them – or worded another way, "bisect the angle of all possible returns."

28 If pulled out wide by your opponent's dink, the best shot may very well be an "around-the-post (ATP)" shot. Remember, the ball does not have to travel back over the net. It can, indeed, legally go "around" the net post – and even below the height of the net.

29 The lob serve is a great change-up serve that forces the returner to generate their own power. This serve also adds variety to your repertoire and can be used to set up future, harder serves.

30 Anticipate and play the percentages. The net is higher at the post and lower at the center. Use this knowledge to your advantage and play high-percentage pickleball.

About the Author

Teresa is thankful to have been raised in a Christian home. She accepted Jesus Christ as her personal Savior at an early age. She attended church and Bible studies all throughout her life. After high school, she studied at a Christian Bible school for 1 year, then went on to receive her Bachelor's degree from Central Michigan University.

Teresa co-founded PickleballMAX with her husband, Todd, in 2015. Over the years, Teresa has developed websites, created pickleball content, helped with pickleball clinics, and helped manage pickleball tournaments.

WEBSITES

PickleballMAX.com
PickleballUserReviews.com

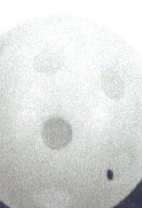